Heart, Mind, & Soul Reflections

Christina Esau-Whitmer

Halo ●●●●
Publishing International

Paperback ISBN: 978-1-61244-086-6
Library of Congress Control Number: 2012913421

Printed in the United States of America

Halo ● ● ● ●   Published by Halo Publishing International
Publishing International   AP# 726
P.O Box 60326
Houston, Texas 77205
Toll Free 1-877-705-9647
Website: www.halopublishing.com
E-mail: contact@halopublishing.com

Dedicated to God

With special thanks to my awesome family for their care, love and patience, Mark Zuckerberg for helping to be the catalyst which helped me realize I could take my writing off of the closet floor and expose it into the sunshine, priceless Soul Friends who encourage, teach, and inspire me in countless ways every day, Dr. Wayne Dyer, Under the Willow Tree Photography, Karean Chapman for noticing and being inspired by my writing in the first place and helping make Halo Publishing a realized dream, &, last; but never least, every fan @ Heart, Mind, & Soul Reflections on facebook. Without each of those early "Likes," I would not have seen what God already saw. Every click, comment, or message has been and will always be highly appreciated. You are all Angels among Angels. Thank you from the bottom of my humbled heart, mind, & soul, always.

Let your life be illuminated with only brilliant light,

Your heart echo joy,

Your mind cascade with God's relaxing clarity,

Your soul renew with the energizing power of faith and Hope,

As you live God's purposes for your life.

Give to give.

Focus on your own internal loving divine light,

Realize God's energy is always available to enhance your Presence,

Right here,

Right now.

Just invite Jesus to rest beside you,

God will always arrive.

Accept this as your expanding miraculous truth,

While asking for His Holy guidance.

The more you do,

The more divine purposes for your life will begin coming True,

Reassuring that God's love is eternal like no other,

Answering our every want,

&

Need within the beauty of innermost stillness.

Explore the treasures waiting to be uncovered within the promises hidden within your soul.

God wants us to call Him with anything,

No special way to talk,

Just let your words form,

Maybe a conversation out loud,

Or within your head,

Surrendering whatever is on your heart, mind and soul in
The moment.

No wrong or right,

I promise.

*May all your intentions turn into better
realities than you could ever imagine.*

God answers every prayer,

Allow your whole being to be calmed with this knowing,

Create within yourself gentle and mindful breathing,

Relaxing into an alignment with your highest self;

Praying with sincere heartfelt and loving intention.

Listening for God's response;

The answer arriving.

Ask truth to manifest with crystal clear understanding,

Thankful for the answers no matter what,

Allowing God's will to also become your own,

Humbly awed by this automatic connection to the Magnificent God residing within each of us,

Honest prayer,

Forever a reminder we really have never been alone.

*Practice forgiving yourself the
way God has already forgiven you.*

The Spirit of you,

The Spirit of me,

The Spirit waiting to be alive in everybody;

All of us connected beautifully,

Manifested from all of God's resounding glory.

Our lives able to interact nonjudgmentally,

Living joyfully,

Helping each other strive to reach our bests;

Existing to help each other discover God's gifts,

Demonstrating God's love for each other safely,

Naturally,

Just let it be.

We resonate with the love we feel
flowing within others, as ourselves.

There is a sublime sweetness waiting for you in soulful
Silence,

Allow God's melodic serenade to carry you along the gentle
Heartbeat of destiny's rhythmic callings,

Go ahead,

Indulging in the simple goodness of your miraculous
Surroundings:

Everywhere,

Nowhere,

All around,

The light within you sought,

Found.

Our lives mirror the reflections of
how we perceive God's infinite love.

Through God,

I seek heavenly contentment on earth,

Through God my needs, wants and connections unfold
Unceasingly through His design every time,

Not mine,

God's love pours contentment into my heart, mind, soul and
Body,

Each blessing,

A gift of sacredness wrapped in the serene beauty of
Contentment;

I have learned to call each of them,

When I am blessed to have one occur,

A divine miracle,

&

The ability to recognize the blessing disguised as a miracle,

Divinity within itself.

Inward to live peacefully outward.

Dear God,

Please take away my careless pride.

Flutter it away on forever's wings,

Guide me to be a more loving me,

Showing me how to choose to have no more weaknesses;

Allow Your needs for my life to quickly become my own.

Please increase my faith, hope and love toward your world.

Allow me to bring both outer and inner peace to Your Magnificence,

Only You know my heart, soul, mind and body like no other:

My every want, need, dream, purpose and desire.

Thank You for everything seen,

Everything gracefully changing within me invisibly,

You are the true source of love's positive power.

Thanking You will never be enough,

But it is all I have to offer from the bottom of my heart's soul,

This tearfully joy stained "Thank You,"

From forever.

*God's love is always ready to cascade
over you with unconditional healing.*

Surround any and all perceived darkness with the most
Beautiful white light you can imagine,

Relax,

Breathing in,

Breathing out,

Imagine gorgeous illuminations engulfing all disappearing
Periphery shadows,

Any lingering dreariness beckoning to drain your soul is now
Leaving,

All gloom ending,

What you feel now glistens from God's pure unconditional
Loving light,

Remaining stresses rushing off into oblivion where nothing,
But goodness waits to welcome them,

All whisked away from you into the heavens where they will
Stay,

You are safe in God's warming radiance,

Prayer,

Always able to enlighten you with pure love's glow;

Returning your heart, mind, soul, and body exponentially
Rejuvenated,

Ready for more.

Just pray.

Every lesson is occurring,

Or occurred for a reason,

Even though we may not understand God's proposed
Purposes at the time,

Always some significance to obtain,

Sustain,

Or we risk repeating the divine lesson again.

Again?

Yes,

Sacred eternal lessons meant for us specifically,

Collectively,

Lessons for our full comprehension now or later,

Always hold on a little longer for the meanings within each
Lesson.

Hold on please,

No matter what,

It will all make sense for the most awesome good later,

Use your free will to trust God's plan for your life;

God will never let you down,

Even if you feel He has,

This is normal,

Please do not let yourself down either,

There is always a divine plan within each lesson waiting to
Reveal more,

Let your lesson teach you,

Hold on to receive the entire magnificent life God has Planned for you.

What you choose to do will always be what happened.

Our thoughts become our realities,

Revealing whom we are choosing to be in each moment,

Privately or publicly,

We choose our thoughts,

Our intentions becoming connections,

With the power of choice directing our destines at all times,

We have the divine ability to enhance our opportunities for Abundance through God's generosity,

Abundance increasing more as we choose to share Selflessly with others,

Enabling others to help themselves;

People we may not ever meet face to face,

But have already met or assisted,

Mind to mind,

Heart to heart,

Soul to soul where authentic living is truly lived,

Many people depend on us to increase our God given Potentials,

To unearth what God planted within us long before we were Conceived,

Recognizing the beauty offered in the now,

Harmonizing regardless of imagined differences in this Gigantic,

Yet in so many ways,

Small world we get to all share,

Us,

God's Universal family.

You automatically extend your
invisible peace to others.

Thoughts are our hidden treasures,

Revealing a myriad of emotions,

Dreams,

&

Our potentials in our most honest moments,

What are your thoughts revealing in this very moment?

Awesome!

Mmm…or not,

We already possess the power with God's blessing to Manifest extraordinary miracles for our planet,

Yes, you and I are perfect for this calling.

Choose your thoughts and actions lovingly to help miracles Come into fruition,

Believe miracles have already begun unfolding;

Know God has the ability to heal hearts, minds, souls and Bodies.

Believe to transfer God's extraordinary gifts,

Surrendering to receiving inner tranquility,

The power of God's energy setting you on an illuminated Journey.

For we are always one loving thought away from aiding Each other's healing.

We were created by a Creator who expects us to create through the highest forms of love.

We are surrounded by miracles,

Look around.

Did you?

I mean really take in the view,

Your eyes to read this page,

Or listen as it is being read.

Amazing!

Miracles unfolded and unfolding,

Miracles have simply never stopped arriving.

You can choose to be an instrument of peace at any time,

Helping miracles unfold through beautiful lighted peace,

Receive God.

Letting Him know you are devoted to being a willing vessel,

Connected to the infinite recognition of epiphany's power;

Ready to begin developing who your authentic self longs to
Become.

Trusting the revelations God's answers will provide when
You listen,

Remaining somehow undaunted,

Yet, overwhelmingly thankful as you help miracles unfold for
Others

And for you,

Embracing each sacred symbol God shows you of His
Divine wisdom and love.

The purest thing to choose never sways.

Sing the song your heart longs to share.

No worries if no one is present to hear,

What matters is the love you create while playing it,

Freeing your passion to mix energetically through your
Metaphorical instrument.

Notice yourself directing your heaven sent love along,

Your overwhelming goodness flowing,

Exquisitely serenading our beautiful planet;

Expanding your thinking.

Elevate the way you find yourself behaving,

Transforming what you are drawn to touching,

The way you may begin lightly walking,

The confident pitch in your talking;

Be ready for the multitude of ways your purposes begin to
Help you begin living authentically, Fully breathing.

Again, or truly for the first time…maybe,

God inviting you on a quest to orchestrate your next
Inspiring songs,

Your best life's show.

*Let your sincerest heart choose the notes
your mind and soul will play for a lifetime.*

Cast your mind's eye upon the beam that flickers.

Its glitz is God's playful wink hoping you will draw closer,

Inviting you consciously to magnify the passionate
Intersections calling to you along your soul's joyful journey.

To contemplate life outside of your imagination's imagination,

To touch beyond feel,

To delve beyond exposed depths,

A human more than always "doing,"

Choosing to "just be" in silence.

A genesis of calmness washing over you in instants of
Shimmering awareness,

Each satori,

God's Holy Spirit empowering you,

Energizing you to acknowledge total awareness;

Inspiring you to pull yourself forward.

These rays of hope warming you brilliantly,

Soul powered by the love offered in this moment,

And the promises illuminated by your destiny.

Know God only has AwesomAntastic
plans for your life.

Where is God?

What is God?

God is everywhere,

Everything you are,

And infinitely more.

God resides within you.

It is truly that simple,

Complex.

Be still.

Allowing your being to focus,

Able to be swept away by the Universe's calming presence;

Ready to view the tiniest to most colossal of God's
Blessings while we're still on His planet.

Bravely committing to experience each intense raw flavor of
Emotion,

Willingly celebrating each wondrous layer of our illuminated
Existence free from judgment,

Appreciating moments as they are unveiled;

Trusting that God will invisibly and visibly sustain you
Through every circumstance.

Accepting worries waste valuable joyous energy,

Through listening awakened,

More aware each every day,

You are becoming pure positive light energy,

Metaphorically, ready to walk, skip and jump alongside the

Rest of the world,

Gliding when you can.

Spiritually travelling God's chosen highway,

Paths you encourage God to choose for you now,

A heavenly interdependence.

Understanding more than ever,

You never have been alone,

A regular peace manifesting,

Radiating gracefully from you now,

Peace pouring from you synergistically.

This is real,

You are not dreaming.

This is your higher self-resonating,

Automatically, you offer Spirit's pureness to other souls you
Feel.

Often, without speaking,

Always from loyal honesty,

Humbled heart service to those aware and unaware on their
Amazing soul journeys,

Remembering,

Honoring, it is God's light illuminating within and from you,
Always,

Not your own,

No accident or coincidence placing you exactly where you
Need to be,

God's actions strictly,

God guiding you triumphantly,

Explaining where to extend a healing hand.

God's whispers of love,

Enabling you to be a faithful server however He originally
Planned.

*In a moment's notice, secret treasures wait
beneath your uncovered awareness.*

The truth is a priceless gift,

Please offer it with gentle gracefulness,

Always with some resounding benefit,

Knowing you will receive a sacred gift in the present,

And so will the other.

Be the peace you wish the world to seek.

You are exquisite because God created you.

God created gorgeous,

Simplicity's charisma,

Abstract beauty;

The sun radiating a multitude of shining blessings upon your
Eagerly hungry face.

The splendor of you so delicate like the softness found only
In the folds of a newborn baby's delicate skin;

The intelligence of you exuding loving ecstasy.

You carry this soul beauty within you always;

Let nothing take it away.

Just like God's grace,

Never disappearing,

Recognize God's energy flowing abundantly around you.

God's love is our ultimate beauty;

Wear it well.

Be beautiful, beautifully you.

Whatever chose to hurt you in the past is finished,

You hold the choice to release it,

You have all of the power now,

Release its ugliness.

For within its severe gruesomeness I promise there are
Treasured gifts,

Gifts buried there by God,

Willing to be uncovered.

You are exquisitely valuable under all of the pain and
Lingering suffering,

Please accept, understand and know this.

Accept this as your unconditional truth,

You are beautiful through and through,

This is so incredibly true,

Own it Dear One.

Nothing you need hide from anymore,

You are the grown up, Victor,

Allow God to help your radiant light shine through you onto
Others in need of your healing help.

Allow God to heal you wholly.

God created you gracefully strong,

Exquisitely strong through each wanted and needed healing
You have experienced.

You are infinitely changed through God's caring desires,

Evolving quickly each day when your heart, mind and soul

Remain open.

Each day something miraculous unveiled within you,

For brave,

Beautiful,

Now healed you,

Let your soul own it.

End your love affair with fear.

Nothing stays,

Everything goes,

Nothing is everything,

Everything is nothing,

Same Universe,

Nothing goes,

Everything stays,

Illusion is time,

Time is illusion,

Stay active while being still,

Active while detaching,

Attach to continue journeying into God's promises of infinity,

Holy eternity,

Everything.

*Trust in the truth of the beauty
that surrounds you.*

Come dance,

Come sing with me,

Even if only in your mind.

God's phenomenal sacredness is alive awesomely.

We are all potential instruments of God's joyous peace,

As the Universe wishes us all to be.

Each of us a unique sound within God's sacred symphony,

Connecting through our loving energy,

God is alive!

*Dust your Angel wings off and fly, Baby! Soar
with your beautifully soul-powered energy!*

Become your soul,

The light God longs for you to become;

Align with the higher frequencies of energy available to you,

Those sublime echoes from heaven calling your free will,

Prized glimpses of God's destiny for your life,

Higher energies blessing your heart, mind, soul and body.

You are not "imagining things,"

Allow your awareness to mature into humble wisdom,

As your thoughts elevate from beliefs into knowing.

Continue to pray for holy guidance,

Thankful for receiving only divine answers,

God's wholesome love emanating from your being.

Share it with the world you meet.

Your passions are the bridges
to your inner freedom.

Just for a few moments,

Live as if today is your last.

Perhaps you will slow down.

What do you want to view that you have not yet?

How will you choose to spend your time, maybe more
Mindfully?

Will there be more reasons to your rhyme than before?

Do you truly understand now there has truly never been any
Reason to keep "score"?

Will you move to the "next place" in peace?

Rest assured,

Many days are probably left for all of us to spiritually
Encounter.

Let every day encourage us,

Create us more mindful, peaceful, stronger,

Many more days lovingly to endure the beauty surrounding
Us when we allow it to shine through Us.

May we continue or begin never to take one breath for
Granted,

Or the breaths of those around us.

Appreciating the bouquet represented by each day we have
Been given,

Making the time to notice tiny details,

Breathing deep thanksgiving for everything;

Knowing each day is another opportunity for an awesome
Glimpse upon God's miracles.

Exploring through our heart, mind and souls' eyes,

Reconnecting to the miracles we have already experienced Here on earth;

Willing to comprehend more miracles are already in loving Motion.

Strive to live in the gift of each moment,

Thankful for the possibilities wrapped in any gifts of a Tomorrow.

Thankful to know to be thankful.

We mirror the experiences in our inner world,

Every moment of every day.

What do you touch?

What do you see?

What do you hear?

What do you feel?

What do you taste?

What do you embrace?

What do you avoid?

Why?

Why not?

We are all connecting each moment of every day,

Or not,

With something,

With someone.

Choosing to connect with something,

Or someone,

Or not.

Each of us a joyous miracle in every conceivable way,

No one better than the next,

Each one striving,

A little at the current moment, or a lot,

Not judged by anyone with success,

Truths to surface only for God and for that person;

God encouraging us to let Him in.

To mirror experiences of unconditional love for everyone,

Our Universe dressed in magnificent lessons and soulful Disguises,

Connecting,

Reconnecting us to the longing within each of us to harness God's promises;

To accept God's brilliantly reciprocated love fully.

We are everyone.

Dear God,

Please forgive us for taking so much for granted,

Our lives,

The air we breathe,

The wonderful people we meet,

The awesome gifts placed within in us;

Treasures in front of us that we blindly miss.

We have no time to make time to be calm from our self-
Created noises,

Lost in our addiction to hurry up and hurry,

Because we seem to wind up thinking somewhere during
Each day,

That we, ultimately, know what is best;

Masking out any hope of hearing from You in calming
Silence.

Amen

*As you write your life's story, autograph
each page with tender gladness.*

Be still

And know the Holy Spirit wants to form your heart, mind, Soul and body with a gentle Strengthening gracefulness,

Your life, built solely of your own devices over time, can Become hardened; frigid,

Let God's healing presence soothe your racing mind,

Your mind, stressed, begins to close with clutter,

Allow the miracles awaiting you in this life to become Available to you,

Mystifying you as they change your life into more than you Could ever dream,

Lest your soul spiral into a familiar dark abyss crying out From a disease labeled "more, more, More" or "I just don't Care."

Your whole life is a blessing.

You are a blessing to so many,

Please understand this,

One moment at a time,

Day by day.

Choose endless gratuity for just being in our world for this Short stay,

With a childlike eagerness to experience God's plan,

Joy always to live your important life.

Stop. Appreciate everything just as it is right now.

I do nothing to deserve your uplifting strength,

The unconditional warmth you always offer me;

Nothing so remarkable to sustain our heavenly friendship.

Your calm beckons me to admit my shadows.

Your essence silently invites me to radiate with simple purity.

Your innate wisdom supports my deepest knowing,

Encouraging a myriad of purposes for my being.

Sublimely symbiotic we have become,

Our union signifies where two authentic selves strive
Together;

We communicate as destiny allows,

Each conversation mindfully,

Heartfelt and deep.

And some,

Just as mindless as our childishness will allow.

My unconditional admiration for you reaching deeper than
Any ocean,

Our Soulship is like a pleasant,

Easy dream always coming true;

Never taken for granted,

Meaning so much infinitely,

Until my last breath,

Our friendship warms my soul completely.

My most sincere hope my friend is that our friendship
Warms your soul, too.

*Time magically disintegrates
between Soul Friends.*

Make time to embrace some silence just for you.

Go away from the noises, sounds, and distractions of each
Day,

Or turn them off,

You will be okay.

You will more than survive silence,

I promise.

Make time to softly be away within your heart, mind and
Soul,

Relaxing into your own body's dimensions,

Just you;

Step away into your own definition of soothing silences,

Wherever,

Allowing yourself to be swept away.

Go ahead,

Free yourself into sweet silence,

Breathe in,

Breathe out,

Be still,

No special skills.

Listening as you go within to locate your highest self,

Learning to ponder what your heart, mind, and soul long to
Reveal to you,

Go for a walk within your soul.

Inner peace is being able to smile even when no one else is around and just smiling because you were created such a special you.

You can access God through the noisy or the tranquil,

No required special "skills."

Be willing to open your Spirit,

Your mind;

Invite quiet time with the Universe,

Luxuriousness,

Just the two of you,

Majestic at best.

Remember,

God never rests,

Never needs a break,

No appointment,

No reservation,

And it is never too late.

You are a sacred space.

Consider making time to be thankful for the people you walk
By on the street,

The people you hold the door open for,

The birds flying gracefully over the head you have been
Granted;

Thankful for whatever is below your feet.

Babies trying to communicate with their crying,

The hustle in the being of everything,

Make time to be thankful for having this experience as a
Human being.

We all have the same amount of time in one day,

Be thankful you know how to use your time wisely.

Learn to make time "freeze" for you,

Living responsibly balanced with a sort of sunshine carefree,

Creating the peace you wish to live among in our world.

Thanking those Angels, who have helped and will help you;

Understanding that soul strings connect us all.

We are what we give.

As the observer in your own life,

Realize the joy offered in every moment of your existence.

Every moment offers you the potential to choose how your
Next moments will be affected.

Consider creating all your moments with a wondrous
Mixture of divine intentions.

You are in essence,

The music,

The words,

The numbers,

The art,

The science,

The love,

The light,

&

All things in between.

You are your choices.

You are your miracles unfolding constantly.

It is a wonder anyone who has discovered this
Metacognition sleeps!

*Be present, knowing you are already
a majestic gift the world needs.*

Surrender to God's surreal silence.

Collapsing into the universe's warming safe stillness,

Lift up your soul with simple sunny bliss;

Give into the longing of a forever favorite reminisce.

Diving again into sweet stillness,

Your inner being arising aware of everything.

Senses now with supernova strength,

Hearing everything within God's stunning silences,

Welcome to real change,

Your whole life is changing,

Changed.

*Allow the turbulence of change to create
constant thankfulness in your soul.*

God is alive!

God is alive inside you,

Inside of me:

Ready to become alive within everybody,

Living within everything seen and unseen,

Living, breathing, feeling within heart, mind, soul and body.

Near or far becoming obsolete,

Holy connections communicating with the beauty of the Brightest stars,

Dismissing the darkness hovering over our earthly lessons;

Leaving us blessed beyond our wildest earthly imaginations,

Transforming us while inhabiting miraculous Angelic spaces.

God is alive!

Such an important truth,

God is always the vibrant love flowing through,

And around you.

Allow yourself to feel it,

No doubt forever changed by it,

God is alive!

Listen to the light of your inner voice sooner, rather than later.

The mirror lovingly captures my reflection,

Reflecting back what I had given to our world thus far;

How I had chosen to shape what has been bestowed upon Me.

Now staring into my mind's sacred eye,

I eventually capture an almost unexplainable blissful white Light.

Feeling the slowing of my strong and vulnerable beating heart,

Accepting an arriving awareness within the light;

Reminding me with inspiring humbleness my priceless life Has never been,

Never will be,

And was never intended to be entirely my own,

Always overwhelmed since little,

Consumed by the sensitive compassion God caringly Packed into my soul.

Relaxing into the brightness, I heard a voice clearly whisper To me,

"Slow down, child; still, you are closer to home than you Know,"

Soul gazing miracles within.

Life's wonders work to weave our
soul threads of love together.

Congratulations!

You have been blessed with another day to experience the Light of God's joy.

Choose to more than just exist Beyond robotic surviving;

Loving joy into each moment,

Willing to refill life's metaphorical cup.

Peacefully replenishing your unique God given vessel,

Filling it with all things spiritually pleasing to you;

Find the beauty to be discovered in a moment spent in Honest elation,

Savoring each moment of each day with appreciation no Matter your surroundings,

Research your inner linings because your life is happening Right now,

Your life representing a clear or cloudy crystal designing Depending on a multitude of choices.

Be a healthy vessel others may admire, pour and drink from,

Knowing we are only responsible for the reflections our lives Reflect,

Never the perceptions.

My! What a beautiful cup you were given!

The greatest opportunities seem to masquerade down life's runway, flaunting as great problems before their magnificent unveilings.

Ask God to increase your awareness with readiness,

Asking to be connected only with the positive gifts offered
By loving authentic Spiritual Ones.

Ask God to increase the power of the light residing within you,

To increase your divine awareness of the lessons, symbols
And teachers available in your life;

Understanding we are all each other's teachers.

Teachers appearing when the proverbial student is able to
Trust the solid revelations,

Some teachers will stay with us for a while,

Some will seem to go.

All sharing critical answers to the lessons hidden within our
Life's winding roads,

Revealing heavenly universal messages required for us in
This dimension,

For our temporary paths here,

Our specific spiritual guides here to guide us along,

Not all aware of their powerful intentions.

Some disguised as earthly Angels helping us help ourselves
Unearth the priceless gift within a Lesson,

Expecting us to trust they have arrived when they do.

Allow peace to connect you to all the joy that awaits you,
Especially through any heartache.

Journeying forward through life thankful,

Helping others just as much or even more than others help
You.

That is what every earthly Angel who has ever helped
Another is destined lovingly to continue.

*I want to thank you, whether you are a reason,
a season, or a lifetime in my life. Thank you from
the bottom of my heart to the highest elevation
of my soul. Thank you for being you.*

Arrange yourself,

Collect yourself into your freely evolving phenomenal mosaic,

Advancing forward, backward, all around,

Seeming to float in midair,

Pieces of peace connecting even before your genesis;

Connecting you here.

You never leave you,

Never will,

This seeming rising and falling of your essence meant to be,

God expects you to untangle your imagined unbearable
Burdens onto His Spirit,

All.

In your weakest weak, please remember your gifts of
Strength,

Release negativity,

Imagine yourself already thriving in ethereal peace,

Believe every catalyst you will ever need in your life is
Already on its celestial way to help you Thrive.

Listen in tranquility for God's heavenly assistance,

Trusting wholeheartedly in His brilliance,

His free energy resides within you minute to minute,

No recharging ever necessary,

Just call upon it.

Pieces of life's puzzle specific to you,

Always willing to interlock with magnetic undeniable

Unconditional love,

Feel this precious energy's claim on your heart, mind, soul
And body whenever you choose to connect to its bliss.

Remain willing to let God help you arrange shifting
Awareness in constant patience,

Your whole life stepping up with higher purposes.

*Choose in each moment to make a divine
positive difference with your energy.*

Life is full of lessons.

Some lessons blissful,

Some unbelievable,

Some lessons painful;

Some excruciatingly crucial.

Some lessons?

Just lessons.

Some lessons, though, you may wonder "what the bleep did That come for?"

Some you will wake up years later and be able to realize,

"OH! I get it now!"

Life can become even more awesome,

More freeing when you realize you get to choose your every Priority, thought and emotion.

Our days are granted with lessons;

Each lesson gift-wrapped uniquely,

Usually ready to humble our egos to their metaphorical Knees.

The Universe's way of keeping us on our toes,

Teaching us patience,

Propelling us to grow;

To care about other living entities,

Not only ourselves.

Encouraging us to pause during a lesson, and when a Lesson seems finally finished,

Each lesson with the ability to catapult current reality into
Something sound.

Believe to receive God's meanings within your lessons
Quickly,

To let the Universe's light shine upon your willingness to
Accept each message gracefully,

Perhaps reflecting on what you are thankful for from lessons
Already learned upon your heart, mind and soul before
Resting.

Welcoming the ability to identify new lessons as they appear,

Thankful to be the awesomantastic you God designed you
To be even before the womb;

Thankful for another day in life's classroom.

*Follow what is echoing from your soul to your
heart because your mind is trying to communicate
something vitally important. Just listen.*

Love yourself no matter what.

Love yourself for striving,

Especially when it may seem like you are nowhere near Arriving,

Even when those around you cannot comprehend the Reasons for your shifting,

For the passion in your reasons,

For your wanting to stop and appreciate,

Or to want to keep going and to keep celebrating.

To continuously being called to give back to the precious Spaces between the gaps,

You are hearing and honoring the echoes your heart, mind And soul has heard so many times before.

You must ultimately give yourself the freedom to answer to You.

The "you" God longs for you to allow yourself to free utilizing His light:

To cultivate the higher purposes within your heart's passions.

It is really just a question of "when" you will choose to do this,

Because as you may have noted,

The echoes recorded in our soul's symphony

Keep getting clearer,

Never truly leaving.

Please choose to take action with the divine gifts you have Been given.

Start now,

Rather than later.

Decorate your destinations with questions so your future will shine.

Some things are not meant to be,

Not always as our human eyes would like to foresee them,

But everything happens for a reason,

On its own purpose,

In its own divine season.

Shine God's light on imagined fears.

Not resonating with someone at the moment? Good!

Yes, you read that correctly.

For those are the individuals we have the most to learn from.

They represent lessons we still need to accomplish:

The turmoil, disdain, heartache;

All are disguised as blessings.

Learn, so you can move on.

Blessings are spiritual catalysts for us to learn the
Necessary beauty of forgiveness.

Forgiveness upon ourselves for allowing our suffering to
Continue too long,

Mighty catalysts into the quantum healing can commence,

Filling us with eternal thankfulness for discovering a
Plethora of secret gifts.

We are worth it and so are they,

Because being separate is always a dangerous illusion.

We are all connected,

Brothers and sisters all along,

When you love yourself unconditionally, you will stop driving
Yourself metaphorically crazy.

Love begets love,

Do unto me if you are nice to yourself, please,

And I will try to do the same.

It will be a lifelong process that none of us humans ever
Masters.

Be willing to learn from each lesson as it comes,

Learning to forgive quickly and sincerely,

Letting all go,

But do not lose the lesson's content,

Lest, life have you repeating the same one.

Only this time,

The old lesson will appear in the form of someone,

Or surroundings only seeming "new."

There is an indescribable peace,
in first, viewing each other as souls.

Know how much you are worth,

Never settling in your own heart, mind, soul or body;

Accepting with full grace the Universe always brings about
Situations that will result in our Ultimate bests.

Sometimes, we knowingly and unknowingly muddy our own
Waters.

Practice patience every,

Every little bit shows others and yourself that you will not
Support settling.

Strive for the excellence innately locked inside of us, which
Is why we crave it,

Or maybe we are striving to regain what we once had back,

That happens.

Those of us striving to be the "always better" souls we can
Be,

For ourselves, for those we serve around us, ultimately, for
God,

Striving to become more conscientious of what is reflected
From our soul mirrors,

We begin arriving on God's purposes for our lives when we
Seek His light from within.

No more views toward the past with disdain,

Seeing only goodness laced with information for our soul's
Balancing.

Old wounds crying out with negativity are comforted only
With sincere joy now,

Old patterns have long lost their original negative soothing

Comforts,

We are illuminated wholly by holy divine guidance.

Having surrendered into this new life,

Elevated through awakening,

Leaving toxicity behind,

Resolving never to forget the lessons gleaned from the Learning,

Thankful for every past, present and any future moments;

Each moment left on the earth to learn something new, Sacred,

Illuminated by the conclusion of each lesson we now know Was veiled as a gift,

To create us stronger.

Go within to discover the brilliant light of God reaching to connect us all as One, again.

Surround yourself with your sacred God given inner light,

Your inner light,

Meant to shine through you,

Surround you,

For you to use.

Be careful of those who might not be able to illuminate in Your company.

Armor your heart, mind and soul with love's purest Illumination,

Your joy emanates.

Stay mindful,

Exit attempts by others for an egotistical dual,

Knowing who you are each day,

When to help,

When to walk away,

Your inner and outer light guiding you,

Truth's light there to guide you,

Always.

Allow only authentic people into the center of your sacred heart, mind & soul.

You are a beautifully radiating blessing,

The treasures buried within your intelligences are
Dynamically infinite,

Believe it,

Know it,

Receiving them with sincere thankfulness.

The beauty of God's love able to flow naturally from you,

Others sense it too,

May all in your presence be prepared to be blessed with
Excellence.

By God's honest caring wisdom, which is manifesting,

Evolving your being daily,

Your positive light influencing,

&

Encouraging others to elevate into their highest radiance, too.

*In every moment, our choices reflect
the kind of influence we want to have
upon the world around us.*

Remember to welcome God into your presence,

Anytime,

Just surrender all unneeded earthly dramatic habits to Him.

I invite you to believe miracles have already begun unfolding,

Majestic miracles meant to bond you with your eternal
Glowing brilliance-

Miracles, my friend!

Allow yourself to become whom you were created to
Become all along through God.

In the here and now,

Keep doing what you already do,

Or try it.

A belief is just a belief until you know.

It is in flashing moments we are often most tested,

So it is in moments we must learn to recall our deepest
Awareness;

Most able to be mindful,

Most able to slow down or accelerate,

Most able to consciously breathe through any perceived
Threat,

Believing strength is simple for us.

Breathing on,

Imagining the end of the situation has already occurred in
Purest measure,

A calm resolve to continue living life doing more than mere
Existing,

Craving God's abundant higher energy to connect with and
Lift us daily,

Enduring anything with healthy boundaries,

Greeting each new day with our proverbial Angel wings
Dusted off and wide open;

Ready to fly into the day producing more light,

Because time and time again,

The light of love offers itself as the ultimate reciprocal
Perpetual worthy prize.

Soulful beginnings have no endings.

Surround yourself with Soul Friends,

Sincere Sisters and Brothers,

Ones consistently willing, gently and lovingly, holding you to
The standards of your highest potentials,

The ones always accepting you as you perfectly are,

And who make it so easy for you to accept yourself, too.

Friends seemed designed just for you and you for them,

Those who make an effort to get to know the authentic you
Deep down,

Allowing you into their heart of hearts,

Knowings of knowings;

Surfaces parallel to their inner beings.

The more you get to know each other,

The more soulful each meeting.

Friends who always know what to do,

What to say,

What to write

Or

When to do or say nothing.

Silence with them sublime,

A friendship just so complete,

They always seem to have a plethora of time for you no
Matter what,

Or they will get back to you soon.

Heartstring friends connect invisibly,

No need for anyone else to see,

Because the higher spirit energy connecting them with you
Reigns silently,

Eternally,

Forever together,

Destined friends.

*Every day it is happening, Earth Angels, managing
to squeeze their beautiful wings through thresholds
somewhere, everywhere, somehow!*

Believe in Angels,

All kinds of Angels,

All around you,

It is true.

For they are there hoping to encourage you along your Magical journey.

Believe in the grace of their miracles through God's power.

They are waiting,

Just waiting for you to allow their powerful loving energies to Transform you,

So true.

*Cultivate a mind full of loving
thoughts, feelings and actions.*

Dear God,

Please take my pain,
Take my tears,
Take my anger,
My fears;
Cast them far away.
Help me advance with joy into new days,

Where I am safe
Feeling the power of Your love,
Whole again;
Rested in knowing only You transcend everything.

Thank you for hearing my sincerest words,

My call.

Amen

*Allow silence to sweetly unclutter
your soul into sublime stillness.*

Dear God,

Please,

Allow patience to come easily to me,
To listen more readily to what You want for my life.
Hold me when I think I am lonely,
And while I am experiencing greatness in flow,
Gently remind me, please, You are the reason I can
Experience such bliss.

You are all I need throughout each day and night.

You are the reason my light shines bright.

Amen

Your inner light has no boundaries.

Dear God,

Thank you for the gift of thankfulness,

The ability to become sincerely thankful for Your eternal Spirit and amazing grace;

For every lesson that teaches us to draw nearer to You for Guidance, ultimate peace and ultimately heaven's eternal Entrance.

With Love,

Your Children

*Begin your entrance into inner
sanctity though delicious silence.*

Thank you for seeing into the hidden depths of my
Vulnerable heart;

For understanding it is only my shadow I wish to depart.

Miraculously,

Rises another divine start,

Coinciding with destiny's prerecorded chart.

Me and my shadow learning to dance with higher energy
Seeking only You,

Each dance slowly evolving into works of Your metaphysical
Art.

Thank You, thank you, thank you for the rest of my life.

*Sometimes the strongest evidence of
strength is being able to ask for help.*

Thank you for all of the beauty surrounding me.

The beauty to be discovered in all You grant me daily,

Bare feet in blades of dewy green grass,

Or just grass underneath my tippy toes,

I will adore it!

Sunsets still burned into my awed imagination,

The warmth of love whenever I am reminded to just pull You Closer;

The light and promises of Your love already glowing within Me,

More than enough,

Simply,

&

Most graciously,

You give to us,

As we need,

In quantities to be measured by only thankful hearts,

Murmuring, "More than enough,"

Always.

*Choose to know you have already
been fabulously blessed!*

Thank you for always accepting me.

Sometimes, I get lost,

But You are always aware of what I need or want,

Packaging what is best for my life in a way that is "not of This world;"

Reminding me to remain true to the essence of the truth in My soul.

Thank you for never giving up on me,

When so many times a situation immediately looked Helpless.

I only stay balanced through Your divine guidance,

Standing strong,

After You help pick me back up.

I know I am a speck among specks,

Forever blessed to have You helping me shine again,

For I do nothing of importance without You,

Nothing on my own,

Shining among all your other diamonds.

*Be gentle with yourself and watch
yourself grow gentle with others.*

Life, so fragile,

Yet, so strong,

Rewind thinking "everything" seems wrong.

Soul feeling sluggishly corrupt?

It is never time to give up.

Always time to mindfully pause,

Stop to rest,

You are the worthy cause.

Silence any perfectionist requests,

Quiet your inner storms by seeking inner balance,

Awaken refreshed,

Forever knowing you are because of the Universe's sincere Grace;

You were created more than worth the elegant best of the Exceedingly best,

Always remember this.

*Choose to be the radiant rippling miracle God
already created you to be within this ocean
of life we all must lead.*

Lost in God's plans,
Take refuge in knowing you are never alone,
Never defeated,
Though some days,
We all hang our head low.

Please do not for too long,

Raise your head up,

You must remain strong.

You are strong,

Your soul is counting on you,

So many others are too.

Others you may not even know about,

Pulling you forward,
Listen to the light,

That is God speaking,

Trying to remind you of the destiny planned for you.

Look up,

Dear One,

Look up,

Your miracle has already begun.

Kick your imagined fears to the curb, Baby!

When we meet on the paths of life,

Or in the pages of this book,

May my inner light already be positively emanating brightly,

Revealing God's true colors through me;

Also, encouraging you to reveal your truest hues too.

Peace has downloaded into the air,

Can you feel it here, there and everywhere?

I do, I really do, Just now!

Not yet?

Well, maybe you will,

Because what you read is what you get.

As we meet,

I am me;

May we always leave warmed by each other's sheer ease
At honesty.

Each of us yearning for a little more time together and you
Know what,

Maybe that is what revealing one's true colors is all about
My true Soul Sister or Brother.

All of us remaining after meeting with a little healthy
Yearning to meet again,

I look forward to meeting you again,

Or someday,

I really do.

Transcend your soul into all its glory where it longs to be.

Beauty siphons through our human spirits;

I challenge you to practice embracing each brilliant glimpse
Of God's beauty as if it were going To be your last.

Memorize the human spirit enjoying magnificence in all its
Glory flying toward you fast,

Each human a beam of light streaming into your presence.

Be willing to meet each soul with warming goodness,

The kind you feel when your heart, mind, soul and body
Cannot help but feel when you Recognize they are alive,

Living on divine purpose.

What are you experiencing?

No attachments to anything but truth,

Pure freedom,

God's love flowing freely because you have allowed a
Perfect powerful grace to enter your Heart's sacred
Tenderness.

Enjoy this challenge,

Knowing these experiences will benefit you daily.

This lightness you are feeling,

Need not go away,

Appreciation does not have to be bliss in passing.

Welcome,

You

Are

Quickly

Becoming

An

Instrument

Of

Enlightened

Peace.

Strive, dream, want, be, just be you,
because you are enough, no matter what.

Consider we are all equal,

Forfeiting futile comparisons of "us" vs. "them" thinking.

Your soul's quest is to guide your heart where it longs to land,

To help bridge the distance to mindful truths each day,

Brilliant soul nudging at your heart to remain open no matter
What,

Culminating all things into an acceptance of life's required
Lessons.

Sincerest gratitude automatically multiplying for all "beings,"

All people breathtaking because God created them.

Our human natures,

Human preferences,

Humans striving to be embraced on a unilateral level no
Matter their race,

Recognized with respect,

No labels needed.

The lesson's call?

Each one of us priceless,

Irreplaceable,

Unconditional caring and love the only ingredient truly ever
Needed.

*You are the tattoo on my heart, mind, and soul I
would never wish to remove.*

Be Still,

&

In the stillness know God.

Accept God reigns within us as a powerful radiant light,

Shining as bright love,

Surrounding us and protecting us,

Expecting us to call on Him at any time.

Know God never leaves us,

God knows our names,

Longing to have a meaningful relationship with each one of Us while we still can.

Let love.

If there's someone you love,

Please tell them now.

Make sure they understand you think they are more than
"Great."

Hold out your heart to be seen, heard and read,

Thankful you made the opportunity to make someone's day
Even more meaningful,

By being you,

Extending your soul's honesty.

*Living in the moment and living for the
moment are two completely different ideals.*

Remain true to what consistently beckons to you;
Love yourself no matter where your heart directs you.

Are these God's directions?
Know your soul will carry you through,
Always;
Let your motivation be the catalyst to your action.

Allow your soul to carry through.

Your soul is your home.

Miracles,

Unfolding perfectly in every moment,

Beyond what our imaginations can see,

Love,

&

Light,

Illuminating the grandiose infinitely.

Go for a walk in the light of your soul.

God puts you where you are supposed to be,
Feel it,
Believe it,
Know it,
Allowing the Universe to work its unforgettable magic
Through you every time.

Go within to discover how we have
all always been brilliantly, One.

Your thoughts make you,
Reveal you,
Create you.
Be aware of what you are thinking,
Entertaining awesomely uplifting ideas;

Knowing the light of your energy helps create more of the
Same,

Abundantly.

Enjoy the answers you will find
in the silent ride of your mind.

Light a bridge extinguishing the past,
Illuminate my now,
&
Any future bright.

May she bring rewarding challenges,
Sincere humility until my last breath.
Help me be worthy,

&

Lovingly more than capable to serve those put onto my path.

I love you, no matter what. Love, God.

When you love others,

You love something about yourself.

When you love others,

You love something about others you wish you possessed
Within yourself.

When you love others,

You love something about others you may already possess
And not realize yet.

When you judge others,

You only judge yourself.

When you judge others,

You need to make yourself feel better in the present
Moment about your own fear.

When you judge others,

You separate yourself further with your imagined fears,

Separating yourself from the liberation calming your original
Heart's upheaval.

When you accept others,

You accept yourself.

When you accept yourself,

You accept others.

When you accept others,

You accept we are all connected,

&

Eventually,

Beautifully,

You may begin to see those metaphorical dots

When connected out of an existing healthy self love,

Can and do form healthy and long lasting relationships,

Peace.

*Eternity would never be long enough to
get lost in the joy your smile brings me.*

When the road your soul has been longing for beckons, you
Will know,

Trust your inner wisdom,

Believing in the celestial pureness that created you,

God's Holy Spirit,

Always available to help you improve your spiritual
Character and personality.

Take the roads as they appear,

Remembering to remain patient and thankful.

Let them sooth your soul's honest purposed passions,

Knowing it may not be an easy haul,

Yet, sometimes,

The challenge adds even more value to what God calls you
To do.

*Feed your soul with the awesome
goodness of natural gratitude.*

Sparkle your soul with gladness,

No matter what has happened.

Learn it is only part of life's seeming madness.

Don't let your life be dampened,

Strive,

Dream,

Want,

Be,

Because you are already enough.

Sometimes just "being" is what is needed to heal,

To feel.

Appreciate today as if it was your last,

Enjoying each cleansing breath,

No matter what happens,

Always striving,

Believing deep down you are already perfect,

Because you were created perfectly in His image.

*Choose to view yourself with God's
resounding compassion and love.*

Some people just resonate with our heart, mind, and soul
Automatically,

Reminding us of how magical life can be,

More than mere cooperation,

Sheer loving;

Joyous chemistry.

Thank you God,

For the days when you remind us of how blessed we are to
Still be here to experience this,

To be aware of your free resonating blessings,

Which seem to soar out of nowhere and into our hearts.

Such pure soul cleansing,

Fountains of peace seemingly heaped upon us in each
Other's company,

Forever carried within the very essence of who we are
Becoming,

People disguised as Angels who help make our world a
Better place,

Even if for just a few moments.

Thank you God for such simple,

Yet, intricate gifts.

Trust in the sheer intensity of illuminated wisdom.

Never put yourself on clearance for another person.

Know you are never half of a person,

Somehow to be thought of or treated as "damaged goods,"

No matter what has happened to you,

Or have chosen to do in the past.

Take solace within God's forgiving, unconditionally loving,
Healing hands;

Welcome God's healing silences to rescue your heart, mind,
Soul and body,

So you can take peaceful,

Needed action.

Please, rejoin us,

We miss you,

Us, the ones who still love you from the bottom of our hearts,

The ones who will never leave you,

Even if you, metaphorically, push us.

We want to try to understand even if there is no way we can.

We do understand you are simply priceless,

Priceless.

Please, hear this,

Remember and…

Keep it as a truth for you,

Because you are always,

Always in every moment,

More than enough,

Promise.

You make my heart smile.

You are never alone.

Allow love to enter into every crevice of your imagined
Illuminating golden space.

Unhappiness is a myth created by an ego that wishes to
Force you into more darkness,

Please do not continue to venture there,

You are so much classier than that.

God's love is true,

Meant for you.

Let His love calm any and all of your fears right now,

Right this very moment as you read this.

Let the warmth of His Holy Spirit encapsulate you,

Healing you in this very moment,

Pulling you up into the highest of highs to stay with Him,

Because God never leaves you.

You are never alone, really,

You never have been;

No reason to ever believe that,

My Friend.

Love in my heart even closer than it appears.

Dear God,

Please forgive us for believing we know what Your world Needs.

After all, this is Your world,

Your Galaxy,

Please help us do Your will with the lives You have so Graciously granted us.

Increase with abundance our abilities to shine Your Everlasting Light,

Increasing in us undying patience, strength and Unconditional loving energy toward ourselves

And all you will, and would have us meet.

Please guide us and protect us unconditionally always.

We know enough to know You are the only One who can Make our lives complete through Your inspired plans.

We can follow our own ideas until we die if we wish,

Or live now knowing You are fully willing to help us direct Our moments with unwavering;

Undying clarity,

Something more than faith.

We feel Your presence,

Thank You for continuing to mold us into instruments of Peace:

Super-sized, gigantic, big, medium, small, tiny, miniscule,

You carry no scale.

We are forever humbled by Your awesome miraculous

Grace.

Amen

We are a reflection of our confidence in God.

You mean everything to me.

The way you teach me,

The way you reach me,

The way you listen incessantly;

The way you are so very patient with me,

Thank you from now until we finally meet.

You mean everything to me.

Everything infinitely,

Thank you is all I can humbly say.

Thank you until we meet face to face,

Spirit to Spirit,

Somewhere far away from here someday.

You mean everything to me.

Ask God to create you to be the person He longs for you to be.

Surrender and forgive yourself,

It is a process,

Take your time,

Or make it fast,

Whatever you choose is up to you.

Know you are more than worthy.

You chose what you chose,

Whatever it was,

It is over now.

I get you choose to let it still haunt you,

That on some level it still serves you,

But you have to consciously choose to stop allowing it to
Rule you.

Wake up, kindly and choose to stop punishing yourself,

Or someone else will right now.

That is your powerful life altering momentary choice to make,

Choose whichever one will bring you the peace you deserve,

You do deserve peace, you know,

No matter what some erroneous voice in your head may
Keep droning.

Until you have time travel at your convenience,

You cannot go back to change things,

And, yes, everything happens for a reason.

My Friend, please choose to forgive yourself,

If God can forgive you . . .

Really, it is past time to surrender it all to God.

Let Him handle it from now on;

Apologizing to ourselves frees us.

Truly forgive yourself this moment,

Just do it,

Let yourself live forgiven,

No matter what has transpired,

Yes,

You deserve to.

You don't have to, you get to.

Please, do not dry your tears.

No,

Not yet,

Let them fall,

For they are heaven sent.

Allow them to cleanse every part of your soul,

Your aching heart,

Your numbed mind,

&

Your entire being that just wishes to unwind.

Do not dry your tears,

Not just yet,

Let them fall,

Falling on you wet,

Wet with renewing hope, love and the miracles promised in Surrendering;

Surrender to yourself all that you try to be master of.

Let your tears fall,

Wipe away a million reasons to hide,

Welcome to who you are suppose to be becoming,

Welcome the authentic world your tears washed off so you Can now see,

Unveiled from deep inside you,

Your illuminating essence,

Shining the truth on all you wish to become,

You,

A sacredly strong rejuvenated entity.

*Value yourself, & you will attract more
loving & enlightened people to you.*

Offer your kindness to everyone.
You have noticed someone in need for a reason.
Not politically correct?
Probably all the more reason to do so.

Use your divine wisdom,

Offer your kindness to everyone;

You have noticed someone in need for a reason.

*Each of my friends represents an
energetic peace to my soulful evolution.*

No one is more deserving than another of God's grace.

All are equal in God's heart.

I am no better than you;

You are no better than me.

God loves us all unconditionally,

No boundaries needed with Supernatural love.

Replace your fear with prayer.

Sometimes it is so difficult to be in this world,

So difficult because I know not to be "of this world,"

So difficult to witness what I have always seen.

Doesn't anyone care?

Don't just walk on by, please,

Don't walk on by everyone with all of those cares now, just
There,

It has been going on forever,

It will go on after me.

Doesn't anyone care?

Don't walk on by,

Please because you are the difference,

You there, choosing to not see,

You choosing to be busy.

Don't walk on by,

Don't drive on by,

Don't click on by,

That is your soul you are walking, driving and clicking by.

Please, go back for all of the heart-filled opportunities that
Await you,

Need you.

You have to care,

Don't you?

The world more than needs someone just like you,

Just like us.

Christina Esau-Whitmer

Your warmth is my sunshine.

.

Nothing, absolutely, nothing is ever lost.

Energy only changes form,

Please know this in your time of heartfelt need.

Embrace this while the pain visits you now,

Believing,

Knowing,

Accepting wholeheartedly,

Eventually,

That everything is on divine purpose,

Always.

*Our hearts are mirrors reflecting God's
love onto the world we all share.*

Allow Jesus' light to elucidate your core with optimism,

Alleviate your mind's alleged shadows,

&

Exalt your healing presence,

As you walk with Him from now on.

Lean on Him to become your best friend,

Through each turning path of this life,

&

Beyond eternity,

Holding His loving,

Caring,

Forgiving hand in cherished knowing highest faith.

Your timeless presence etches
a serene smile upon my being.

Your whole life is your song,

Turn it up,

Replaying the scrumptious parts,

Turn down the unneeded ones,

Change the notes that need changing.

Cherish the symphony recorded within your heart, mind, soul and body,

Understanding the notes are suppose to change all the time.

Their interchanges becoming uniquely sublime sometimes,

In flux just part of each one of life's treasures,

The purest essence of your music thriving magnificently,

Endlessly,

&

Beyond each timed measure.

Dance even if everyone is looking!

May you know that nothing can ever persuade the light
Inside of you to diminish,

Nothing,

Even when it feels like the weight of the world has now
Fallen upon you,

Carry on strong,

Knowing that God has already provided you with everything
You need to carry love's purpose Through.

*Willing minds seek enlightenment through
the reflections mirrored within their souls.*

Your strength carries the body that holds my spirit,

Your excellent mind challenges me to reckon beyond the Sun's sublime rays,

Your spirit permeates through me,

I am simply lost in the beauty of you,

Honored to call you friend.

Truth gracefully and patiently
illuminates our destinies.

God will place you exactly where you are suppose to be
Every time,

Feel it,

Believe it,

Know it;

Allowing the Universe to work unforgettable healing
Miracles through you unceasingly.

*God is the masterpiece of all masterpieces
allowing us to be His artists.*

If someone or something has hurt you,

Know everything in our Universe is always on divine purpose.

Realize you hold the power in every moment to let go of any Negativity,

To envelop the warmth of God's gentle, healing powers.

God's serenely graceful presence ready in a moment's Notice to wash over you,

Cleansing you back again.

The Universe's loving light shining on the hope of Faithfulness,

Very soon you will be more than okay,

Belief becoming knowing,

For your miracle is always unfolding when you become Open-hearted to receiving it.

Peace,

Dear One,

Peace,

As you realize you are beautifully,

Soulfully mended,

As intended.

God transcends everything into perfection.

Appreciate what you do not want,

To understand what you do want;

Sending clear intentioned prayers toward your honest Passions.

Watching God's will manifest into your life,

Enjoy the beauty of miracles unfolding brilliantly before you,

Every time,

When we make the time to align with God's higher sights.

Surprise someone today by saying,
"I'm glad you're here!"

From my soul to your soul,

Perhaps, my words will resonate,

Excavate the heart of your understanding,

Meshing your higher thoughts into my own;

Create an illumination over your inner knowledge.

This book?

God's idea,

Written just for you.

My sincere prayer is you will find something soulful to keep,

Something heartfelt you can call your own.

It has been with enlightenment that it was composed,

May God bless your inner light, always,

With tears of sincerest joy I must go now

But as you know,

One is truly never alone.

Until next time,

Thank you,

All my love.

*True love is a rose petal's touch
as it gathers to your nose.*

CPSIA information can be obtained at www.ICGtesting.com
Printed in the USA
LVOW130617311012

305196LV00005B/223/P